A CARIBOU ALPHABET

written & illustrated by

Mary Beth Owens

The Dog Ear Press, Brunswick, Maine

**A portion of the proceeds from the sale of this book
will go toward the restoration of woodland caribou in Maine.**

Caribou were common in the northern United States as little as 80 years ago. In 1986, a group of citizens formed
the Maine Caribou Transplant Corporation to restore this magnificent species to Maine. In December of that
year, 27 caribou were transported from the Avalon Peninsula in Newfoundland to the University of Maine at
Orono. By 1988 the nursery herd had grown to almost 50. In 1989, at least 25 caribou will be released into
the wilds of northern Maine. About 100 caribou will be released in the subsequent 4 to 5 years. Funding
for this exciting project comes entirely from private contributions. For further information write:
Maine Audubon — Caribou Fund, 118 U.S. Route 1, Falmouth, Maine 04105

This book is officially endorsed by

the Maine Caribou Transplant Project

Printed in the United States of America by Holyoke Lithograph, Springfield, Massachusetts.
Color Separations by Digitran Color Systems Limited, Winooski, Vermont.

Art Director: Sheila Garrett
Editorial Assistants: Alison Daley Stevenson, Nessa Burns   Production Consultant: Jack Leether
Photo references: (newborn) Jack Walas, University of Maine; (reindeer) Dino Sassi, *Lapponia*, Wittet Company, Oslo

10 9 8 7 6 5 4 3

Published in the United States by The Dog Ear Press, 19 Mason Street, Brunswick, Maine 04011
Co-Published in Canada by Firefly Books, 3520 Pharmacy Avenue, Unit 1-C, Scarborough, Ontario M1W 2T8

Library of Congress Cataloging-in-Publication Data

Owens, Mary Beth
A Caribou Alphabet.
Summary: An alphabet book depicting the characteristics and ways of caribou.
1. English language — Alphabet — Juvenile literature.
2. Caribou — Juvenile literature. [1. Caribou. 2. Alphabet] I. Title
PE1155.0925 1988   [E]   88-70631   ISBN 0-937966-25-8

To the sovereign God who is my strength,
who makes my feet like the feet of a deer,
and enables me to go upon the heights.

Habakkuk 3:19

A caribou's **antlers** can grow mighty large

Bulls spar in the autumn to see who's in charge

Caribou **cows** protect calves as they grow

And teach them to **dig** for their food in the snow

An icy **escape** on swift, steady feet

Is rewarded in spring with sweet **foliage** to eat

Grazing on plants that grow close to the ground

Kalmia plants such as labrador tea

Spring's **journey** moves on at a much slower speed

When maddened by **insects** a herd may stampede

Caribou travel in **herds** the year round

Are as tasty a meal as **lichen** can be

Migrating bulls follow trails old and worn

While **newborns** arrive where their mothers were born

Old man's beard is a lichen which hangs from spruce trees

But a **predator's** taste is much harder to please

q

The Canadian **quarter** sports a caribou's head

While **reindeer** pull Laplanders home in a sled

Vigorous **swimmers** of river and stream

Caribou show by their **tracks** where they've been

An **ungulate's** hooves help on every terrain

Itchy **velvet** rubs off and strong antlers remain

Into the wintry **woodland** they go

By MicMac called **xalibu** — "pawer of snow"

Curious **yearlings** find comfort together

Caribou thrive in below **zero** weather

A CARIBOU COMPENDIUM

by Mark McCollough

Antlers — Bull caribou and some cows can grow antlers. The cows use their antlers for protection. Bulls use their antlers to spar with each other during the autumn breeding season. Sometime in winter or early spring the antlers fall off, just like leaves from a tree. In the spring, a new set will grow.

Bulls — Male caribou are called bulls or stags. They are much larger than females and weigh from 200 to 650 pounds. In the autumn, a fully grown bull caribou has majestic bronze antlers which sweep over his head in a graceful arc. His neck is covered by a long, flowing mane. He is very strong from thrashing bushes and fighting with other males. If he is successful in battles with other males, he will stand guard over a group of three to fifteen cows.

Cows — Female caribou are called cows or does. A cow caribou weighs between 150 and 275 pounds. Caribou mothers give birth to only one calf each May or June. The calf follows its mother for a year. During that time, she protects it from predators and teaches it how to survive in the lands of the North.

Dig — In the winter when the snows get deep, it becomes difficult to find food. Caribou gather on ridge-tops where much of the snow is blown away by the wind. Here, they sniff the ground for lichens, grasses and herbs and dig away the snow using their large hoofs.

Escape — Caribou have to be alert for danger. They prefer to gather close together in open areas like bogs, tundra and frozen lakes, where they can detect an approaching bear or wolf at some distance. If a predator approaches, a caribou might give an alarm signal by lifting its head high and putting a hind leg out to one side. Other caribou recognize this signal and prepare to escape. If the predator comes too close, the whole herd takes off at a run, trying to outdistance the danger.

Foliage — Caribou are herbivores, which means they are plant-eating animals. In all, caribou are known to eat 250 kinds of plants, including wild mushrooms. Some of their most common foliage foods include willow, grasses, bunchberry and huckleberry. During the long arctic summer days, caribou feed constantly to build up a layer of fat for the winter. The fat helps keep them warm and provides energy when it is hard to find food in the deep snows.

Graze — Caribou are grazing animals, meaning that most of the time they eat plants that are close to the ground. If you travel in northern Alaska or Canada in the summer, you might see thousands of caribou grazing peacefully on the tundra.

Herd — Caribou spend much of the year in large herds. A migrating herd might stretch for 50 miles and be made up of thousands of animals. Each herd has a leader, usually an older adult female. She leads the migration and finds the best pastures for feeding and resting.

Insects — In the summer, millions of biting insects emerge from shallow ponds on the tundra. About the same time, caribou shed their thick winter coat. Their sparse summer coat is just right for hot summer days, but doesn't provide much protection against the insects. Caribou herds will often panic and run for days to get away from black flies, mosquitoes, warble flies and bot flies. Sometimes they find refuge on a snow-field, or a windy ridge-top. Other times, they travel to the Arctic Ocean to stand in the cool ocean breezes.

Journey — Caribou are constantly on the move to their traditional summering, breeding, wintering and calving areas. For some herds of barren-ground caribou, this yearly journey can be over a thousand miles. A young caribou learns this important migration by following its mother during the first year of life. A mother caribou will return to the place it was born to give birth to its calf.

Kalmia — Kalmia is the name given to the genus of plants that can be found in the wet, cool environment of a bog. Labrador tea, Sheep Laurel and Pale Laurel are a few of the members of the genus, Kalmia, that are a favorite food of caribou.

Lichen — Lichen is a small spongy plant that grows on the shallow soils of the tundra. Some people call it "reindeer moss" or "caribou candy" because the caribou eat it whenever they can. Actually, deer and moose will also eat lichen, but caribou are the only members of the deer family that can live entirely off this unique plant.

Migrate — There are two kinds of caribou: woodland and barren-ground. Barren-ground caribou live in the farthest northern regions of Canada and Alaska. These herds of caribou are on the move year-round. In the spring the cows begin to migrate to their traditional calving areas. The bulls and yearling calves follow at a more leisurely pace. The cows and their new calves continue to move all summer, often 300 miles or more. In autumn, the mature bulls rejoin the herd. After the breeding season, or rut, the herds are again on the move to the wintering areas. In this way, caribou always have enough plants to graze on.

Newborn — Newborn caribou are small — weighing only ten to fifteen pounds — but are up on their feet and nursing within an hour of birth. Within two hours, the calf can teeter after its mother on long spindly legs. A four-day-old caribou can outrun a man and maybe even a wolf. The mother caribou's milk is the richest of any land animal. On this nutritious diet, the calf grows quickly and doubles its weight in just two to three weeks.

Old Man's Beard — Woodland caribou live in the northern forests from Newfoundland to British Columbia. At one time they even flourished in states like Maine, New York and Minnesota. In the winter, woodland caribou often eat Old Man's Beard, a type of lichen that hangs off the branches of spruce and fir trees. This light green lichen got its name because it resembles the scraggly beard of an old man. In the winter, woodland caribou run towards the sound of dead trees falling. They know that these trees are often covered with Old Man's Beard, which makes a tasty feast for hungry caribou.

Predators — Wolves, bears, lynx and people have always hunted caribou. Predators are Nature's way of removing sick and weak animals from the herd, allowing strong and healthy caribou to survive. The Eskimo, Inuit, Lapp and Sami people have been careful hunters, taking only what they need and using all parts of the animal. In recent times, however, some humans have upset this balance by overhunting and disrupting or destroying traditional grazing lands, migratory routes and breeding grounds.

Quarter — Several million caribou still live in the tundra, bogs, barrens and forests of Canada. Canadians have honored caribou as one of the symbols of the country by putting a caribou on the back of the quarter. Other animals on Canadian coins and dollar bills are beavers, robins, loons and kingfishers.

Reindeer — There are slight differences between the caribou of North America and the reindeer of Europe and Asia. Reindeer are generally smaller than North American caribou; some have been tamed and used as work animals. Laplanders, who live in Northern